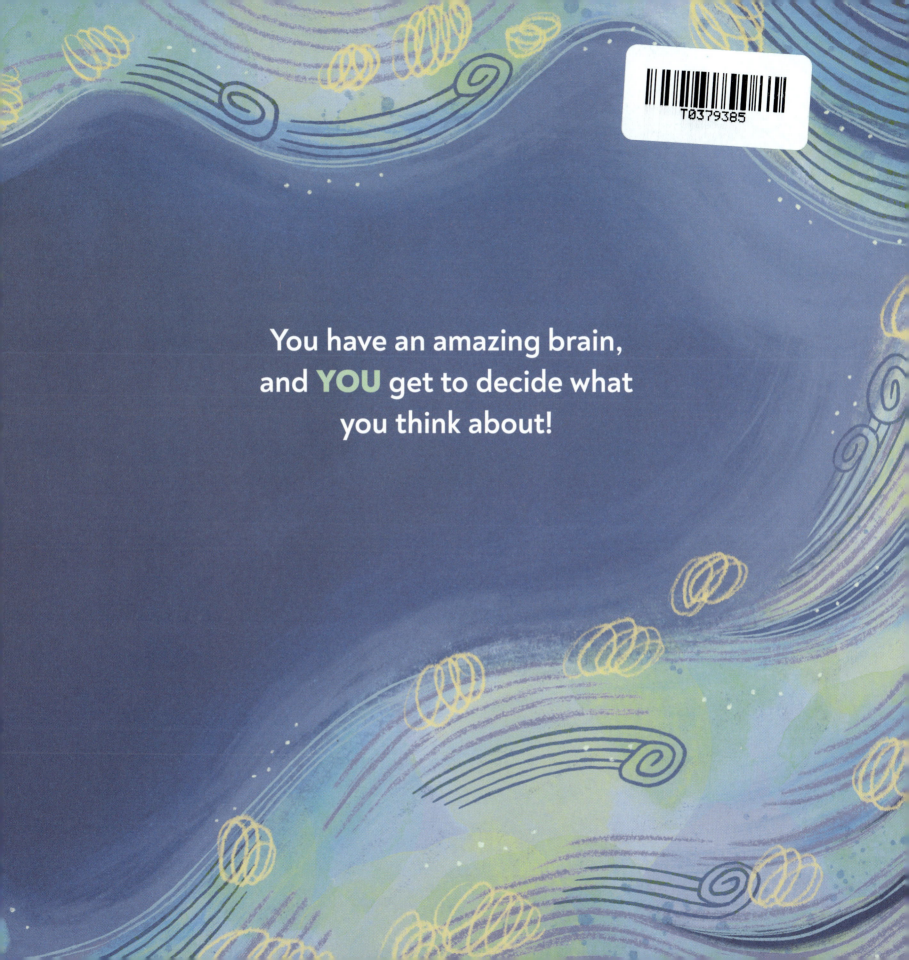

You have an amazing brain, and **YOU** get to decide what you think about!

What to do with your WHIRLY, SWIRLY THOUGHTS

AUTHOR OF *GET OUT OF YOUR HEAD*

JENNIE ALLEN

ILLUSTRATED BY
NADIA GUNAWAN

An Imprint of Thomas Nelson

What to Do with Your Whirly, Swirly Thoughts

© 2025 Jennie Allen Ministries, LLC

Tommy Nelson, PO Box 141000, Nashville, TN 37214

All rights reserved. No portion of this book may be reproduced, stored in a retrieval system, or transmitted in any form or by any means—electronic, mechanical, photocopy, recording, scanning, or other—except for brief quotations in critical reviews or articles, without the prior written permission of the publisher.

Published in Nashville, Tennessee, by Tommy Nelson. Tommy Nelson is an imprint of Thomas Nelson. Thomas Nelson is a registered trademark of HarperCollins Christian Publishing, Inc.

Published in association with Yates & Yates, www.yates2.com.

Tommy Nelson titles may be purchased in bulk for educational, business, fund-raising, or sales promotional use. For information, please email SpecialMarkets@ThomasNelson.com.

Note: This book is intended to provide helpful information about mental health. However, it is not a substitute for professional medical advice, diagnosis, or treatment.

Scripture quotations are taken from the Holy Bible, New International Version®, NIV®. Copyright © 1973, 1978, 1984, 2011 by Biblica, Inc.® Used by permission of Zondervan. All rights reserved worldwide. www.zondervan.com. The "NIV" and "New International Version" are trademarks registered in the United States Patent and Trademark Office by Biblica, Inc.®

ISBN 978-1-4002-5278-7 (audiobook)
ISBN 978-1-4002-4990-9 (eBook)
ISBN 978-1-4002-4986-2 (HC)

Library of Congress Control Number: 2024050569

Written by Jennie Allen

Illustrated by Nadia Gunawan

Printed in Malaysia
25 26 27 28 29 OFF 5 4 3 2 1

Mfr: OFF / Batu Tiga, Malaysia / April 2025 / PO #12260313

Because of Conner, Kate, Caroline, and Cooper. Being your mom is one of my greatest gifts.

A LETTER TO PARENTS

Dear parents, aunties and uncles, grandparents, teachers, Sunday school leaders, and all of you who love the next generation,

Nearly twenty years ago, I found myself smack in the middle of raising a house full of little ones. I wanted to know God for myself and teach my children about who He is. I wanted resources that caused my kids not to just know about God but to also experience His power and His love for them. My greatest prayer was that my kids would have a personal relationship with Jesus.

And as the world changed and anxiety in children continued to rise, I desperately needed a book much like the one you're holding in your hands. These days, our world craves hope and simple language to talk about negative thoughts with kids.

Romans 12:2 says to "be transformed by the renewing of your mind." This means it's possible.

But each person's brain is different. I know that some children bounce back from setbacks easily, while others may ruminate in a negative loop and have to work really hard to get out of that thought pattern. And others may not be able to control their thoughts at all due to developmental impairments or more serious mental illnesses. Still, I believe this book will help most children who struggle with whirly, swirly thoughts by providing practical and biblical tools for taking our thoughts captive. Learning how to manage our thoughts is a big part of our emotional development, and our children need to learn this before they encounter "thought obstacles" that can add to their struggles.

Sometimes anxiety, depression, or the effects of trauma are beyond our control. Please read these words with great compassion. Sometimes we need more help than redirection! Praise God for the help of counselors and doctors.

Choosing our thoughts is a whole new way to live, and it is only possible through God's love and help.

I know that being a kid (and a parent) these days is hard. My prayer is that reading and discussing this book with your kids will bring freedom and health to their thought life and will ultimately point them to the hope we have in Jesus.

Now more than ever, kids need the freedom that Jesus offers their thought lives, and they also need the love of a safe adult who cares about them and shows up for them again and again.

I am cheering you on!
Jennie

Oh, look at all your thoughts in that cute little head of yours!

Sometimes you think **happy** thoughts.
Sometimes you think **angry** thoughts.
Sometimes you think **silly** thoughts.
Sometimes you think **worried** thoughts.

Did you know you have thousands and thousands and thousands of thoughts every day?

What are some of your thoughts right now?

Sometimes your brain fills with exciting thoughts!

When you feel your parents' hugs,

when you remember eating ice cream with a friend,

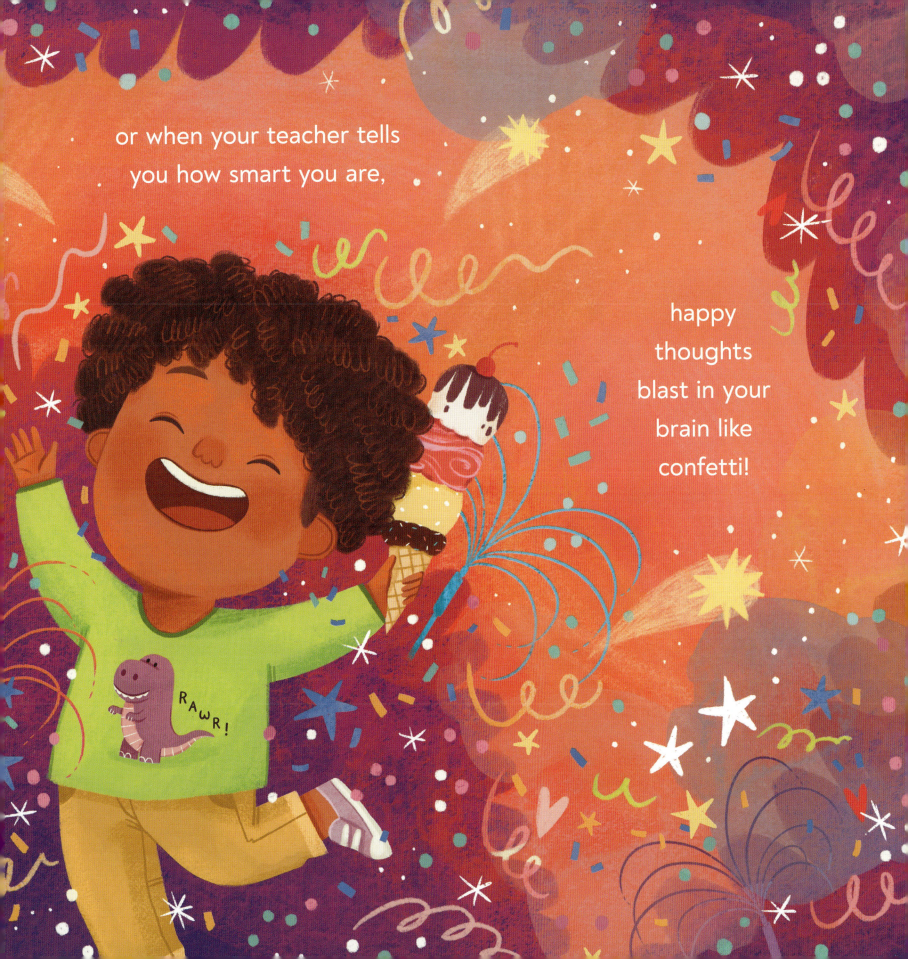

Your amazing brain can create masterpieces.

And it helps you talk to Jesus.

But sometimes your brain fills up with thoughts that make you feel sad or scared.

Like when you make a mistake
or remember how someone hurt you.
Or how you feel lonely and like
no one wants to be your friend.

And you know what? You're not alone!
Even grown-ups sometimes have these thoughts.

Those thoughts can grow so big that they get stuck in your head. They keep whirling and swirling around and crowd out other true thoughts!

You can't finish your art project.

You don't want to play with your friends.

You can't sleep.

And you even get a little cranky!

So what do you do with your whirly, swirly thoughts?

You can train your brain like a muscle! What if your brain could run **100 miles** or lift **100 pounds**? That seems pretty silly, right? But God says we can help our brains get stronger!

Your brain is a wonderful, powerful gift from God. Your brain tells your body how to **move**, your feelings how to **feel**, and your mouth what to **say**. Your brain is the control center for who you are and all you want to do.

And God made YOU the boss of your brain!

You can help train your brain how and what to think.

So whenever your thoughts grow BIG and start to spiral down the way you whirl and swirl down a slide, remember . . .

YOU can tell your thoughts who's boss.

Tell your brain . . .

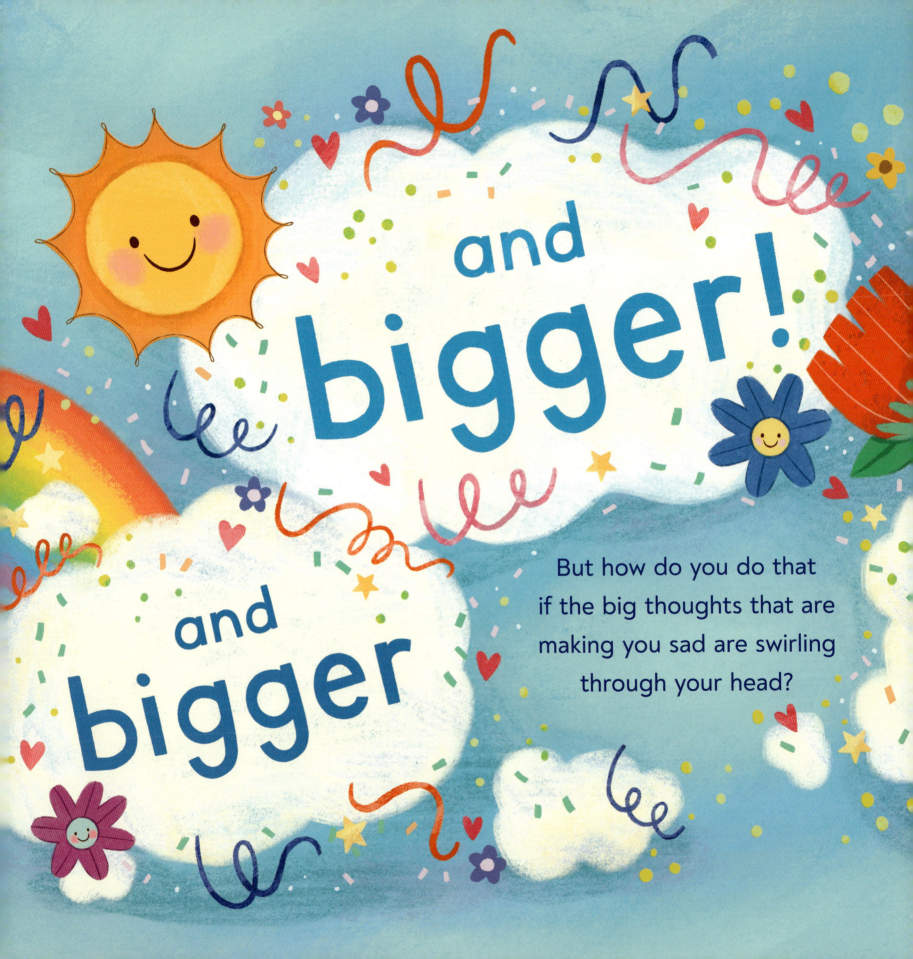

and **bigger!**

and **bigger**

But how do you do that if the big thoughts that are making you sad are swirling through your head?

Did you know you can get out of your head by saying your thoughts out loud?

Tell those whirly, swirly thoughts to God and to the people who love you.

Say a **little**.
Say it **all**.
Say it **fast**.
Say it **slow**.

Say it so those thoughts can **go, go, go**.

Did you know you can get out of
your head by being thankful?

Now you try it!
What are three things you're thankful for?

Thank God for **fun**.
Thank God for **hard**.
Thank God for **ice cream** and
butterflies in your yard.

Did you know you can get out of your head by moving your body?

Instead of letting thoughts whirl and swirl in your brain, your body can whirl and twirl those thoughts out of your head!

Jump on the trampoline, dance to your favorite song, or ride your bike to put those swirly thoughts to bed.

YOU HAVE A CHOICE!

You have God to help you.
You have people who love you.
God loves you.
He sees you.
And He wants you to know
you are never alone.

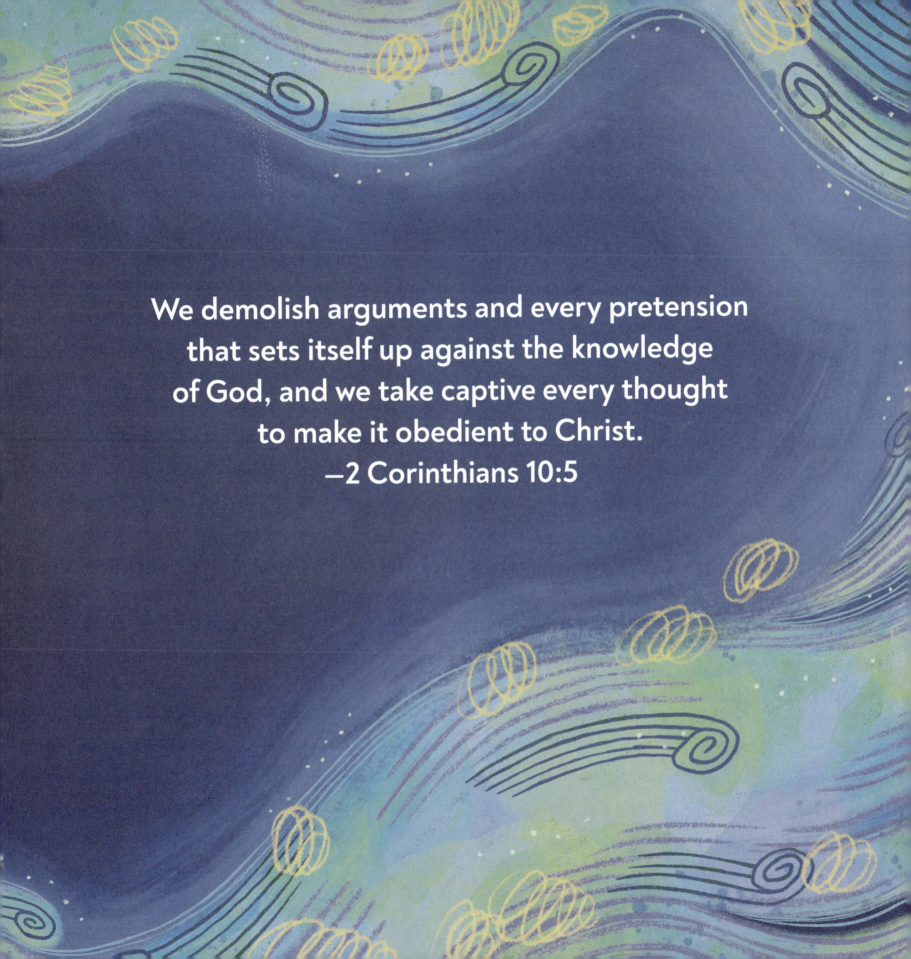

We demolish arguments and every pretension that sets itself up against the knowledge of God, and we take captive every thought to make it obedient to Christ.
—2 Corinthians 10:5

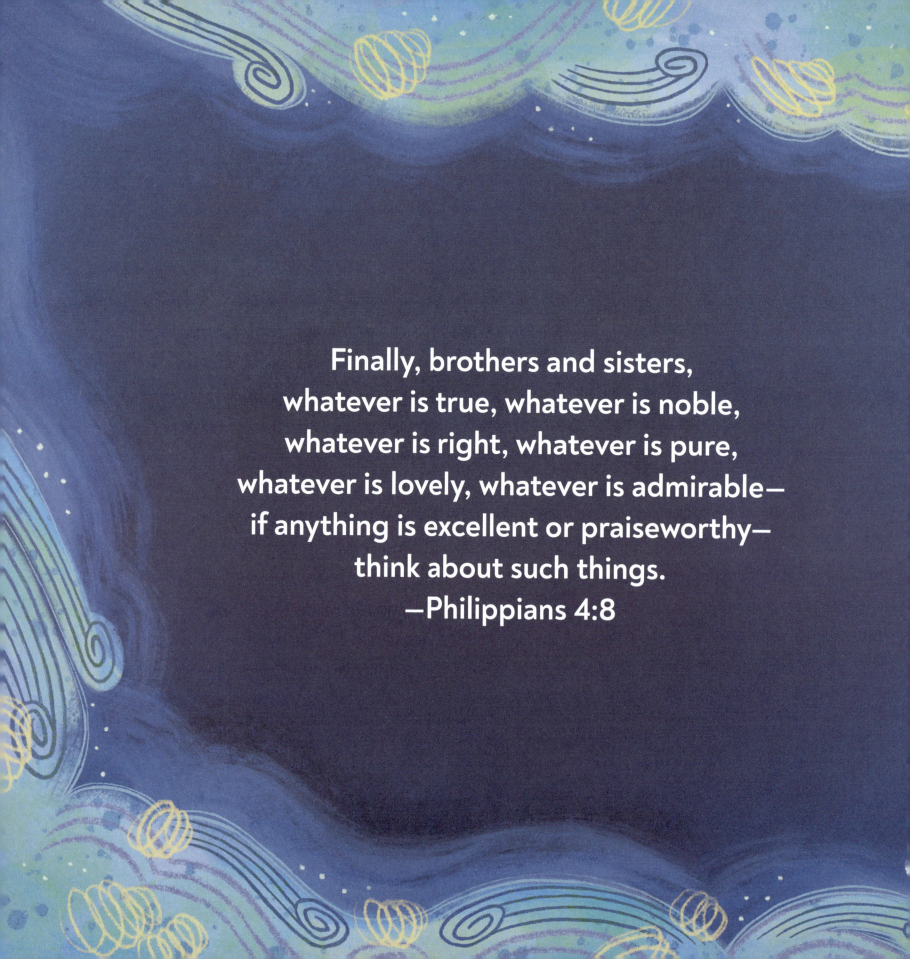

Finally, brothers and sisters,
whatever is true, whatever is noble,
whatever is right, whatever is pure,
whatever is lovely, whatever is admirable—
if anything is excellent or praiseworthy—
think about such things.
—Philippians 4:8